*This book is dedicated not to a person, but to a place, to a piece of land in the State of Israel, a hill overlooking the northwestern shore of the Lake of Galilee, which is called the Mount of Beatitudes. On it a Church was founded, a Church for any and for all men, and the ceremony of foundation was finished with these words, which are for all churches and for all peoples, "Be ye therefore perfect, even as your Father which is in heaven is perfect."*

# A CATHOLIC SPEAKS HIS MIND ON AMERICA'S RELIGIOUS CONFLICT

Thomas Sugrue

HARPER & BROTHERS, NEW YORK

A CATHOLIC SPEAKS HIS MIND ON AMERICA'S RELIGIOUS CONFLICT



*Printed in the United States of America*



D-B

*Library of Congress catalog card number: 52-6283*

criticism vanished from the parent body, the Roman Catholic Church. Four hundred years later, in the latter half of the twentieth century, it is still absent, and the damage its exile has caused within the Church is incalculable, incalculable because there is no way to more than hazard what Catholicism might be today had her rulers not theorized that criticism by Protestantism from without—a criticism expressed continuously and powerfully by the simple fact of Protestantism's existence—made criticism from within too dangerous to tolerate.

The only available technique for judging the matter is therefore negative; the actual condition of the Church today after so long a period of prejudice against self-criticism may perhaps be taken as an indication, at least in some measure, of the health she might be enjoying had she been willing during all this time to regard herself now and then as her friends and communicants saw her. Among those Catholics who dominate the American Church, for example, the things I have said about their kind of Catholicism in the following pages will be denounced as anti-Catholic, when in fact the most cursory examination of these statements will reveal to anyone that they are instead pro-Christian, being based on an affirmation of the metaphysics of the Sermon on the Mount. Thus, if they are indeed anti-Catholic, Catholicism is anti-Christian. Such Catholics as recognize this paradox will wish, of course, to avoid its implication, but they will not agree with me in my conclusions. They will say, with the hurt look of an abandoned fawn, "Why didn't you let somebody else say that? Aren't there enough Protestants pouring criticism on the Church without one of our own adding to it? We're not perfect but we're better than they are, and anyhow, the least we can do is stick together."

My answer to this is that what I have now said is the first thing that in my life I wanted to say, and that it has burned in me steadily since I initially felt its sting in my brain and in my heart. I do not think that any group of people, whoever they may be, should be allowed to employ the Church, a Christian institution founded and maintained for the spiritual task of redeeming mankind, as an instrument for the expression and the exercise of that group's peculiar prejudices, neuroses, personality imperfections, and grudges against life. In America the Church has been used as a vehicle for the social, economic and political ambitions of certain immigrant groups from Europe—Italian, Irish, German, Spanish, French—bent on building themselves from identification as poor foreigners to recognition as middle-class Americans. It is a natural ambition and in no way reprehensible, but it has nothing to do with the purpose of the Church, which is to give sustenance to her faithful in the world of the spirit and to guide them through the labyrinths of the mind and flesh toward God. What has happened because of this unholy alliance of the Church and American free enterprise is bad for the Church and for the American Catholics involved in it.

There is the case, which I know well, of the Irish. In their natural state the Irish are among the very best companions made by God. They are as easy to love as a morning in May; they are amiable, witty, good-humored, and objective about the irritations and unpleasantries of life. Being Irish myself I don't know what I would have done without them. But when they are ambitious and wear the Church as a cloak for that ambition, they depress me and they frighten me.

Many of them are tempted in that direction, and Irish history under the English no doubt gives them a justification for yielding; but the rejection of justification is a mark of the mystic, and an Irishman ought to measure up to that mark. Because he never was able to lick the English is no reason for him to salve his frustration by trying to conquer the Church of Rome and the government of the United States. Things are bad enough in the supposedly separate worlds of religion and politics without that sort of unreason to contend with and to dismember.

There is no doubt that the Irish flavor I found in the Church of my youth—and which thrives in the Church of my maturity to the point of matching, in Catholicism, the power and prosperity of my country among the nations of the earth—came to be there not because of the Irish but because of the Church's moratorium on self-criticism and her allowance of the notion among Catholics that a battle against Protestantism was in progress and would remain in progress until the enemy capitulated. These two points of view are ideal for the paranoid—Irish or German, Italian or Spanish—who cannot endure either blame or responsibility, and who projects his inner tensions outward to the world, which he condemns to the role of enemy. The Church has thus allowed herself to become a refuge for the irrational, the frustrated, the defeated, and any who cannot reach the grapes of the world and decide to hate all those who do. If instead of these points of view the Church had declared to her members that their only obligation as Catholics was to deepen their participation in the ideals of Christianity, she would have drawn to her as defenders and upholders of the faith less of the paranoid and more of the pious, fewer of those who concern themselves with the moral state of others and more of the sort who meditate on the spiritual balance within themselves. But that is an academic supposition, since the majority of the Church's members are born into her embrace; her choice is not what they are by nature; she can only decide what it is she should encourage them to become. If those who feel the need of her power and influence in their personal lives borrow it for this purpose, it is her responsibility if she allows them to do so.

The theory of papal infallibility in matters of faith and morals, for example, is instantly debased when it enters the mind of a paranoid, who adapts it to his personal inability to endure the responsibility of error, and who lives off it as a parasite. The loose supposition that the Church can do no wrong is another example of a misinterpretation prevalent among certain Catholics who are otherwise quite normal people. The amateur theology behind this bit of folklore is varied and optional: God will not let the Church err because she is His chosen vessel; He cannot permit her to err because He founded her Himself, through the personality of His Son, and He cannot go back on His own handiwork; the Church has a divine mission and God by His own rule is not allowed to interfere with it. I found long ago that setting reason against these theories was unwise and brought no positive results. Once I pointed out to a young man of the Church that God had created Lucifer and then allowed him to rebel and to fight against God Himself. The Devil, I also pointed out, was allowed to tempt Jesus. "The Devil," the young man said, "was never a member of the Church."

There is more of this than one would suppose but less than is necessary to give the Church in America a general countenance of spiritual pride. The Irish clergy who dominate the American Church are an intelligent, disciplined lot: they run an efficient organization, and among them are good, wise, and even holy men. But in a society in which it is normal to say, "I admit the man's a saint, but–" they provide what is needed beyond spirituality in order to make good in America. Under their guidance and prodding Catholicism in America has made good. What I have all my life wanted to ask, and what I now do ask–breaking the taboo of self-criticism as I do so–is only this: is it Christianity? If not, then it is not Catholic.

The answer which long ago I found to be true and wanted then to announce is that it is not Christian and that it is therefore not Catholic. I am saying this now, myself, without waiting for someone else to say it–some Prod. I am breaking the taboo because I fear very much that if we American Catholics continue to stick together we shall perish together; if we cover up the rotten apples in our barrel any longer we shall lose the good apples along with the bad. We are becoming so thoroughly disliked for our perversion of Catholicism to an overambitious Americanism that from now on anything—anything at all—can happen.

As I ponder those few Catholics of my acquaintance who will be glad that I have broken the taboo I realize that they are of many racial strains, including certain Irish of both the laity and the clergy. The Irish, as I have said earlier, are a people with almost infinite capacities for charm, intelligence and objectivity. Some in fact are all that the Irish can be, and a few of these I have found and clung to, and will never release. Those of them who are among the clergy are the closest to my heart, for they are the priests who serve the idea of salvation, who oppose evil with persistence but without hysteria, and who regard the Church as an instrument of redemption, not as a spiritual monopoly through which God is obliged to work.

The gentlest and the wisest of them are natives of Eire and students of Maynooth in the days of "Old Walty" McDonald, the great teacher who believed that theology should be dynamic, changing as man himself changed, able always to guide the human mind reasonably and safely from knowledge of itself to knowledge of God. "Old Walty" wrote a book which harmonized Catholic theology with modern science; it was presented as an explanation of the Trinity, and it was called *Motion*. It was sent to Rome and after a careful study at the Vatican it was placed on the Index, the Church's official list of literature forbidden to the faithful. "Old Walty" was not disturbed. Rome, he said, was inhabited solely by "third-rate theologians," incapable of understanding his book, let alone of judging it. He continued to teach at Maynooth and his book remained on the Index.

To the students of "Old Walty" whom I have met—gentlemen and scholars all—and to any who unknown to me inhabit American Catholicism; to my Irish Catholic friends who in this matter are "wid" me and not "agin" me; to any and all Catholics who are inclined toward the notion that religion is an activity of the inner life which reflects itself in the outer life; to my friends among the many Protestant denominations and in the non-Christian religions of Hinduism, Buddhism, Judaism and Islam; and to all Americans of whatever faith, I therefore address the pages which follow. They contain a confession I have wanted to make since first I found the idea of God within me staring out at religious sectarianism in the town where I was born. I am glad that at last I have made it.

THOMAS SUGRUE

*December 9, 1951*
*New York City*

# A CATHOLIC SPEAKS HIS MIND

# PART ONE

As a member of the Roman Catholic Church, into which I was baptized at the age of one month; and as a citizen of the United States, which I became at the hour of my New England birth, I have been since my earliest moments of communal consciousness draped painfully and with little grace across the horns of a dilemma—does my Catholicism interfere with my Americanism, as some non-Catholics are inclined to think, or, as Rome might put it, does my Americanism interfere with my Catholicism?

The dilemma does not pinion me alone; it holds every American Catholic aloft on its points, and has done so for a long time. Normally it is politely ignored, but now and then it draws attention to itself by an incident which commands that it be noticed, that it be observed, and that it be studied. The most recent of these incidents is the announcement by President Truman of his intention to name an ambassador to the Holy See at the Vatican State in Rome. It has brought my dilemma, and that of every American Catholic, to the attention of everyone in the country.

I think, therefore, it is time that I, that American Catholics in general, and that all responsible Americans of whatever sect or denomination, address this dilemma with honesty, with sincerity, and with all the evidence and intelligence which can be mustered, in an effort to discover whether the horns may not be lowered and their prisoners released. Does a totalitarian religious system interfere with a democratic political system? That is the question.

That it may be approached properly and with hope of a true answer it is necessary to dig a little into the question of man himself, into his religious nature, and into the democratic system of government he has evolved for himself here in the United States.

There are two discoveries which every man early in life makes about himself—who he is in relation to other people, and who he is in relation to God. Together these two realizations, once they are in his mind, inspire, stimulate and select a major part of the man's thoughts, actions and efforts. He is continuously at work, so long thereafter as he lives, adjusting one or the other of these relationships—what people think of him and what in his conscience he thinks of himself—improving it when he is able, sustaining it when he is threatened. His success in both areas of labor, one of them external, the other internal, determines and regulates his personality, shaping it into a person at peace with his community and content within himself, or forcing it into the semblance of an anarchist, a malcontent at war with everyone, including his neighbor, his God, and himself.

What a man is on the inside is normally visible from the outside. Who he is in relation to God is reflected in his relationship to men; the condition of his inner life rules by compulsion his attitude as a social being; he is inclined to act toward others in a manner which indicates how he feels toward himself. How he feels toward himself, on the other hand, is influenced by the people he encounters and the persons with whom in daily life he is intimately concerned. If they manifest for him regard and affection he is apt to share in these feelings, giving thus to himself the love he is commanded to give also to his neighbor. The golden rule advises him to do unto others as he would that they do unto him; if he is able to express love toward his fellow man very likely he will express love toward himself, and since love comes from God, as a part of His radiance, when he knows this he will love both himself and his neighbor as part of the single act of allowing God to love him.

The world of relationship with others—the social world—is therefore a testing ground for the world of man's relationship with God. Man himself sits between the two worlds, watching both his actions in society and his activities within himself. He knows that within himself he must win the battles of understanding, morality and discipline which improve his relationship with God and deepen his sensitivity to love; but he also knows that the evidence of his victories can only be demonstrated for others by his thoughts, acts and deeds in the community—and until he is a saint the demonstration of his victories to others is the only way he has of being sure of them himself. He cannot even know that he is a saint except by demonstrating saintliness to other men; as a man gets closer to God his fellow men feel him coming nearer to them. The two worlds of man, then—relationship with God and relationship with other men—are interdependent, and the state of one can be determined by conditions in the other.

It is the function of religion to interpret these two worlds to the man who inhabits them, to evaluate them for him and to demonstrate their interdependency as forces in his personality. If a small boy one day comes upon the fact that he is a member of the poorest family in his block, and that his block is in a slum, he should have at hand the comfort of another identity, in another world, where he is rich rather than poor and where he is not only the equal of everyone, but his superior, being the beloved of God. Theoretically this is so; religion is available to all and preaches its message at least once a week; an American boy, along with the knowledge that he inhabits a democracy in which through diligent effort poverty may be overcome, has offered to him information which states that the kingdom of heaven is within him, that he has but to seek and he will find it, and that the key to its discovery lies in loving God and in loving his fellow man, whoever that fellow man is and whatever his behavior and opinions.

Actually this is *not* so. The American boy who discovers that he is poor and socially underprivileged finds out, usually about the same time, that he is also a Jew, a Catholic, or a Protestant; and this further identity, far from being a compensation for the burden of his economic status, is a weight added to it. It is not, to him, a joyous revelation, a treasure relieving him of all misfortune, an identity making him one not only with the Creator but one with all that is created, so that he is united with, not separated from, all others in the outer world. It is instead another force which separates him from these others; it is a further portion of his relation to other people; it is, like being born poor, something imposed upon him by circumstances about which he was not consulted and over which he had no control. If he is poor and also Jewish, it means only that he is doubly poor; his Jewishness offers him a philosophy and a theology, but most immediately it places on him the weight of anti-Semitism, which demands that he work twice as hard to get half as far in his community, and which shuts him, in his own consciousness if not in theirs, from all Gentiles. If he is Irish and also Catholic, he is doubly alien; his Catholicism tells him he belongs to the "one true Church," but it drops on him in the same breath a "difference" from all other people in the most snobbish of categories, the status of a soul before God. If he is American and also Protestant, he is doubly American, for his Protestantism, giving him as a heritage the freedom to seek God on the wings of his own inspiration—with the guidance of the theology of his particular church—also endows him with a "difference" from Catholics and from Jews, who are Americans, but not in the triple sense of the term—native birth, Anglo-Saxon descent, Protestant religion. In all three cases, thus, the spiritual and compensatory identity of a boy—his discovery of who he is in relation to God—is imposed on him in the form of membership in a particular religious denomination, membership he did not request, but which comes to him along with the color of his eyes and the shape of his nose, from one or both of his parents. It does not introduce him to God, or to the deep gregariousness of the spiritual life; it acquaints him with religious sectarianism, and with the dismal fact that in his relation to God he must through all his life be separated from the majority of his fellow men, whom God has informed him are his brothers, and commanded him to love.

This is the basic failure of religion; by not remaining united it has separated men in their worship of God. In America, where by himself any man may become anything, no man can be spiritually close to another man so long as the two belong to different religious sects and are faithful to the tenets of these sects. They can transcend the limitations of the sects, or they can ignore them, and thus be unlimited in their friendship, but they cannot be sincerely sectarian and spiritually be brothers. In a community it is even difficult to overcome sectarian divisions on a social level; it is easier to remain in one's own group than to follow a friend into his. Yet no people are less sectarian-minded than Americans; they have just not found any other way to seek their relationship with God, and they do not know how—or have not the courage—to tell their religious leaders that what they want and need is religious unity. As a result, religion for Americans, instead of acting as a guide for the inner life and projecting an influence into the outer life, has become a guide for the outer life and projects an influence—sometimes not even that—to the inner life. It is because of this that Jews in America support an Anti-Defamation League and protest against presentations of Shakespeare's *Merchant of*

*Venice*; it is because of this that American Catholics conduct their own schools and cultural organizations, and list their own taboos in the arts and in literature; it is because of this that Protestants are uneasy and apprehensive about a Presidential plan to send an American ambassador to the Vatican. It is not the religious activities of a denomination or sect which cause other denominations and sects to regard it with suspicion; these, under our law of religious freedom, are respected and admired. It is the secular activities of a denomination or sect which set other denominations and sects to eying it askance.

We have, therefore, in the United States, religious freedom, but not religious tolerance. There is an armed truce which goes by the name of religious tolerance, but behind its curtain of manners and hypocrisy the old "differences"–personal opinions translated into secular prejudices–are as raw as ever and as ready for action. All religious roads lead in the end to God, just as all rivers, eventually, reach the sea; pilgrims on these highways know that this is so, and realize that many roads are necessary for the many kinds of people, who begin their spiritual journeys from a multitude of points of view. It is the commanders of the highways who will not have it so; each wants preferential rating for his thoroughfare, and longs to reduce all other turnpikes to the status of tributary. Such sectarian and denominational commanders as are not of these opinions are most apt to be genuinely religious; it is sectarianism–irritating and restrictive in social life, poisonous and frustrating in spiritual life–which marks the defeat of religion and the perversion of its purpose as an aid to man in his search for inner and outer peace, in his desire to be known well by others and to feel well with God.

The fault for this defeat lies in no particular sin, or with no particular group; it is not the rotten fruit of a lust for power among the clergy, or the ruined wheat of lax congregations. It is mainly the result of a normal human limitation, an inability on the part of almost everyone to perceive that the two worlds of man, the inner and the outer, the psychological and the physical, the spiritual and the material, are continuously co-operative and interdependent, but are constructed and governed on systems which are *diametrically opposed to each other*. As both the mystic and the psychologist will testify, the system of the inner world is totalitarian. The "I" of the psychological and spiritual kingdom must be the absolute ruler of that kingdom, a monarch with divine right, a god whose subjects are completely subservient to him, doing only his bidding and seeking neither to coerce him to their point of view nor to rebel against his rule and depose him. A man, in other words, must be master of himself. He can decide to take orders from somebody else, but only he can make that decision. He is not divisible into a committee. He is one person with one ruler–himself.

All of human history, on the other hand, demonstrates irrefutably that this system for the outer world is utterly wrong, bringing misery to all but a single man, allowing for the full development of only one personality in an entire nation. The correct system for the outer world–right if not perfect–is democracy. In democracy each man is free to develop fully his personality, which means that he is given freedom socially and politically, so that within his inner world the "I" which is himself can freely grow into a king with absolute power and with a divine right of rule. This is the interdependency of the two worlds, the interdependency which religion should teach and should labor to maintain.

The necessity for totalitarianism in the inner world is easily explained; it is felt, in fact, by all people, though it is seldom realized by any of them. The "I" of the inner world is confronted by subjects who are really only parts of itself, appearing in the forms of feeling, image and idea. What are actual people in the outer world are in a man's inner world only forms made by his thoughts. He can never know a friend as that friend really is, but only as the friend appears to be by way of his mental impressions of him and his reactions to him. A man's feelings present him with desires, and these obviously should not be allowed to overcome him and possess him, for he will then be, as the mystic and the moralist alike assert, "a slave of desire." A man's images provide him with his memories and his impressions of people, and if the memory and impression of a single person—a parent or teacher or nurse—is a pattern of fear and pain, the image of that person will usurp part of the authority of the "I," and govern certain areas of the inner world by leaping to authority when the "I" comes near them, frightening him off with the same pain and fear which afflicted him when the image first entered his consciousness. A father who frightens a son and strikes him when the boy expresses his intellectual curiosity by taking a watch apart, is apt to remain in his son's mind indefinitely in that image, and go on punishing the boy for intellectual curiosity. The personality of the "I" then appears in its expression to be lame, or eccentric, and is considered neurotic, having lost control of one of its parts. A man's ideas provide him with his sense of balance and structure, of meaning and dynamism, in both the inner and the outer world. If one idea gets control of the "I" and speaks for him, the personality expressed is prejudiced, fanatical, and single-minded, and the man is considered a crackpot.

The governing of the inner world must therefore be a ruthless dictatorship. Often under the guidance of a psychotherapist—an analyst or a psychiatrist—a man discovers that the image of his mother has usurped control over large areas of his inner world, so that many decisions which he thinks he makes for himself are made instead by a picture of his mother stamped on his mind in the years when she actually *was* making decisions for him. He must, then, the analyst or psychiatrist tells him, free himself from the power of this image, and since it is indeed an image, and has no life except the life he gives to it, he is free to kill it. This he can do in a dream, or in a fantasy; so long as the mother-image is destroyed it makes no difference how the deed is accomplished. But the man is by no means free to kill his real mother, his mother in the social world; if he does this he is psychotic, and will be treated as a homicidal maniac. In a milder way the man whose inner world is commanded by desire must conquer that desire on the field where desire is at present victorious; he cannot regain control of himself by preaching against desire in other people. Nor can a man possessed by anti-Semitism return himself to reason by asking other people to join him in hating the Jews.

Yet since the beginning of history men in general and in particular have suffered from this natural mistake: everywhere and at all times the system of the inner world has been extended to the outer world, with invariably disastrous results. Tyrants have tried persistently to capture all of humanity, and all of humanity at times has demonstrated a tendency to submit itself to dictatorship. Self-rule and personal freedom seem almost to be acquired characteristics. It would seem that man in the beginning knew his inner world, and was aware of how it must be governed, but did not know his outer world, and had to learn gradually how to live on the earth as a human being and as a social animal. By habit, and because he knew no better, and because he gave to other people only the value he placed on the images in his dreams—images he was free to kill or enslave—he extended the ruthless totalitarianism of his inner world to the social problems of his outer world. From the beginning, therefore, society had the chieftain who was a god and the shaman who exorcised, conjured against, and otherwise fought the wicked images who threatened the community. Human sacrifice and ritual murder in the outer world were a direct reflection of image-murder in the inner world. The same was true of animal sacrifice, magic and taboos. The dangerous forces of the outer world were contended with as were the dangerous forces of the inner world. A member of a tribe might find himself at any time treated as if he were an image in the mind of another member of the tribe, just because the other member dreamed about him. If he had acted badly in the dream he might be acted upon badly by the dreamer; he might even be killed. Only gradually did man discover that what was inside of him was not necessarily outside of him, that whereas each man had his own inner world, with its problems and anxieties, there was but one outer world, and that in common men had to share its problems and anxieties, co-operating so that each was protected from all others and left free to deal with his inner world as he was able. The shaman slowly developed into the priest, and after a while the judge, the lawyer and the policeman emerged. But it was a long time before the divine right of kings vanished, and after that monarchs stayed on their thrones by right of blood. The last ruler by divine right in the Western world is master of a state only one mile square; but the power and influence of his divine right extend to nearly four hundred million people all over the world. That is why even certain Catholics, devout though they may be, sometimes fear the power of the Pope; they are afraid his rule in religious matters will spill over, as it has in the past, into secular matters.

Jesus did not found a state; He suggested a Church, one through which man might find his way to God. Man had lost much of his original familiarity with the inner world, and had put his effort into learning how to conquer the outer world. Whereas early in his development he had regarded the inhabitants of his inner world as more real than those of his outer world, now he regarded members of the social community as solid entities and the figures of his mind as ghosts and fancies; whereas once the inhabitants of his dreams invaded the community as spirits possessing other men, now other men invaded his dreams and possessed his soul. Jesus reminded His followers of the reality of the inner world, and gave as His teaching—

specifically in the Sermon on the Mount—a technique by which the "I" of the inner world might conquer that world completely. Then, in complete control of all that was contained in himself, the "I" could deliver that self to God. To the outer world—to Caesar—what must be given was to be given. But the technique of success in the outer world was not to be introduced into the inner world, any more than the technique of success in the inner world was to be introduced into the outer world. What went into the belly did not necessarily reach the heart; a dietary law was not the business of the inner world. A man could do many things with his knees and his lips, but these things did not guarantee that he worshiped God; one could not sneak into heaven by the back stair.

He spoke almost always of the inner world; it was to that world that He came, bringing not peace but a sword, to cut father-images from the "I" of their sons, to sever son-images from fathers, to separate mother-images from daughters and daughter-images from mothers. In the inner world those who were not with Him were against Him. His kingdom, He explained to Pilate, was not of this world; to His disciples He spoke of His Father's house, which had many mansions. Then, because He troubled the outer world by speaking of the inner world, the outer world put Him to death in the manner of the inner world. It crucified Him.

It was natural that His Church, as its organization became formal, took on the totalitarian system of the inner life. Early Christianity was genuinely concerned with redemption; early Christians anticipated the return of Jesus within their lifetime, and expected all members of His Church to abandon activity in the outer world in favor of effort in the inner world. When these two phenomena did not occur, and when Rome fell and the Dark Ages moved in on Europe, the Church's totalitarian government, modeled on the system of the inner world, planned as a guide for man's spiritual redemption, extended itself into the outer world. The Popes assumed temporal power, became worldly in their personal lives, and the trouble was on.

A man who represents himself as the "Vicar of Christ on earth" cannot make political deals with emperors, traffic in indulgences, and sell bishoprics to the highest bidder without reducing the general opinion of his spirituality more than a few degrees. Nor can he rule as a king in the outer world without engendering suspicion as to his primacy within his own inner world; power, as both peasant and prince know, corrupts, and absolute power absolutely corrupts. The papacy became a shame and a disgrace to Christendom. As Karl Adam points out in his recent book, *One and Holy*, which is a Catholic examination of the hope for religious unity, "the Renaissance Popes seem to have carried out in their own lives that cult of idolatrous humanism, demonic ambition and unrestrained sensuality which was in many ways bound up with the reawakening of the ancient ideal of manhood." Leo X, for example, found hunting and the theater, as Mr. Adam points out, "more important than Martin Luther and his religious aspirations." At the investiture of Leo X as Pope, "the Most Blessed Sacrament," Mr. Adam reports, "was accompanied by statues of naked pagan gods."[1]

Long before this, however, a "good" Pope, a monk named Hildebrand, who ruled as Gregory VII, and who later was made a saint, set the fuse of the Reformation by declaring that papal power extended into the secular world and could expel unworthy rulers and release from allegiance the subjects of such rulers. Hildebrand ascended the Chair of Peter in 1073, and set out at once to free the Church of simony, to abolish marriage among the clergy, to stop secular rulers from naming bishops and abbots, and to make the general position of the papacy—weakened by careless and worldly Popes—stronger and more respected. He met with heavy opposition from much

[1] Karl Adam, *One and Holy* (Sheed & Ward, 1951), pp. 12, 13.

of the clergy and from most of the secular rulers; he was angered into overusing, and thereby diluting, his power of excommunication. He fought bitterly with the German Emperor Henry IV, excommunicated him, and at Canossa kept him outside the gates for three days, barefoot in the snow and wearing only a penitent's gown. Later Henry took revenge; his army sealed Hildebrand in Rome, and the Pope sent to the Normans for help. They came, and they drove Henry's soldiers away, but they then sacked Rome, burning, looting and raping. After that the Romans hated Hildebrand; for his whim their city had been destroyed.

What Hildebrand claimed for the papacy eventually produced Protestantism. The Church finally launched a Counter Reformation, but the Popes retained some temporal power until the middle of the last century, when the Italian revolution led by Garibaldi did away with the Papal States and made the Vicar of Christ, after 1870, a "prisoner" in the Vatican. Since that time the Popes have been interesting for their interpretation of the place of the Holy See in both worlds, the inner and the outer. Pius IX proclaimed the doctrine of the infallibility of the Pope in matters of faith and morals. Leo XIII spoke out for social justice and seemed a liberal and modern mind. Pius X reversed this stand and condemned "modernism," seeming to head the Church back toward the Middle Ages. Benedict XV reversed *that* stand. Pius XI worked to extend the Church's position as a power independent of protective temporal rulers and mediators; he labored also toward the idea that in their various countries the clergy should develop local loyalties politically and Roman faithfulness religiously. He encouraged the sending of political representatives to Rome. In one of his encyclicals he said of this growing tendency:

This gives us great pleasure, not only on account of the increased authority of the Church, but also on account of the greater glory of its benefices and the experience it gives to all of its inestimable virtues, in bringing to human society all prosperity including civil earthly well-being. For if indeed its direct object is, by Divine command, spiritual and eternal blessings, still, by the close connection of things, it helps the earthly prosperity of individuals and society, as well as if it were instituted for no other end.[2]

This was an indication, phrased somewhat with pride, of a tendency to regard religion in its proper sense as a guide for the inner life and an influence, ethical and moral, in the outer life. The tendency had been developing since 1870, as a habit of withdrawing from politics and concentrating on the development of Catholicism as a world-wide religious organization.

But withdrawal from politics is very nearly impossible for a Pope; Pius XI was an autocratic man who leaned toward dictators; in 1929 he and Mussolini consummated an agreement, Mussolini giving him the Vatican as an independent state, hoping in turn to get papal support for his Fascist ambitions. Pius XII came to power in 1939, in time to preside during the war which wrecked Mussolini and Hitler and pushed Russia into power. He was trained as a diplomat, had served as papal Secretary of State, and since the war has led the Church in its fight against Communism. But now there is rumor that he has become a thorough mystic, that he has even had a vision of the Virgin Mary; he has proclaimed the dogma of the Assumption of Mary, announced the discovery of St. Peter's bones, presided over a Holy Year, and made various statements about marriage, family life and birth control which indicate that he regards sex from the mystic's point of view—as a force which in combination with love propels the mind and heart toward God. Thus he also tends to regard the Church as a guide for the inner world and an influence in the outer world.

Yet in his position as Pope he inherits the scars of his predecessors—the prejudices and suspicions resulting from their

[2] Quoted from William Teeling, *Pope Pius XI and World Affairs* (Frederick A. Stokes Company, 1937), p. 94.

mistakes and their sins—and he is burdened with the results among Catholics of contemporary political crises and catastrophes throughout the world. The collapse of Europe from World War I onward and the rise in wealth and population of the Americas has been a continuous Vatican worry. Support for the Holy See has for thirty years now come largely from the United States. Americans are democratic; what will happen when they control the papacy? Catholicism in the United States is totally nonmystical; it is booming, aggressive, materialistic, socially ambitious, and inclined to use its membership as a paranoid pressure group, threatening anyone who so much as criticizes the way it ties its shoelaces. It gives the immaculately mannered Italian nobles in the Vatican shivers of revulsion. Leo XIII condemned what he called "Americanism" in 1899, and Pius XII in 1950 added this comment:

> We cannot abstain from expressing our preoccupation and our anxiety for those who, on account of the special circumstances of the movement, have become so engulfed in the vortex of external activity that they neglect the chief duty [of the Christian]: his own sanctification. We have already stated publicly in writing that those who presume that the world can be saved by what has rightly been called the "heresy of action" must be made to exercise better judgment.[3]

The Pope's feeling for the materialism of American Catholicism is matched, on the other hand, by American Catholic opinion—articulate but not official—of the Holy Father's coddling of dictatorship in Catholic Spain. The pro-Franco attitude of the Vatican is a heavy load for American Catholics to bear, and one they resent and fear. As one American Catholic expressed it, "I don't want any trouble with the Church, but support of Franco is the point at which I stop being a good Catholic." Some years ago when the governing clergy of a

[3] Quoted from Thomas Merton, *The Ascent to Truth* (Harcourt, Brace and Company, 1951), pp. 5, 6.

Catholic diocesan newspaper interviewed for an editorial position several Catholic newspapermen, they were met by a persistent question. Each applicant said, "Will I have to support Franco editorially? If so I cannot take the job."

The practical reason behind the Vatican's friendship for Franco is simple. Spain is the mother country of many of the South and Central American republics, all of which are Catholic. The people of these countries identify their Catholicism more with Spain than with Rome; their reaction to papal disapproval of Franco might be disastrous for the Vatican. Yet this does not explain what seems like a papal partiality toward Spanish Catholicism and, on the other hand, a discouraging Vatican attitude with reference to certain progressive and liberal tendencies which have sprouted in French Catholicism since the last war. Old suspicions stir easily, and there has never been any evidence that the papacy looked with even mild approval on democracy as a political idea.

Whether the papacy is at present antidemocratic is, however, an academic question. It cannot afford to be. It is fighting against Communism, which is totalitarian, and its allies in this fight are democratic. The Church's members in Europe have fallen by the million to the rule of Russia; in the Western world the majority of her faithful dwell in democracies; should Russia attack in the West armies of Protestant young men—with Catholics and Jews among them—will fight for her. However any Pope may nowadays feel about fashions in government, he must live with, co-operate with, and be supported by, the style called democratic. In the centuries when it had to get along with monarchy the papacy made an ill-advised effort to bring each monarch under its control; it is naturally scrutinized in the present for indications of an attempt to reduce to subservience the governments of democracies.

It is an unlikely prospect at the moment, but as a possibility in the future it cannot be dismissed as absurd, since when Catholics in democratic countries are dominating the Vatican there will necessarily be a compulsion to "advance" the faith in these countries, Catholicism being by its own definition "the one true Church," and man's ideal state, by the same Catholic definition, being a society where the Church and the State are one. This is an intolerable notion except on an *if* basis of complete idealism; if the Church were perfect, and humanity were perfect, all men would be monks and all women would be nuns, and in one mystical generation life on earth would be finished and redemption would be achieved. The tendency of certain secular priests and some Catholic laymen and laywomen to delude themselves into thinking that because of their loyalty to the Church they are as good as monks and nuns, and that redemption proceeds apace when Catholics have influence in government and in culture, creates the revulsion which Protestants feel for the Catholic habit—in the United States specifically—of working and voting to place Catholics in Congress and in high government positions.

Domination of the Vatican by Catholics in democracies is not far off; there is general opinion, in fact, that the deed is already accomplished, and that those who dominate are the American Catholic clergy, the men who deliver to Rome certain of the moneys they collect from the American faithful. It may be a polite domination just now, but where the money comes from there also the orders—gently presented as suggestions—are apt to originate. Before too long there may be an American Pope, with a "summer" residence here and a College of Cardinals packed with American bishops. The government of the United States might then find itself sending an ambassador to an American citizen, who as head of the "one true Church" would rule in matters of faith and morals over twenty-five millions of Catholics bent on extending their influence, and his, in the native country of the ambassador, the Pope, and the twenty-five millions of Catholics. As a final irony, this American Pope would almost undoubtedly be Irish.

What is presented to American Protestantism is therefore a mixed problem; Catholicism in Rome and in Europe regards Catholicism in the United States as materialistic and overzealous in its pursuit of success in the external aspects of religion—real estate, bank balances, institutions and organizations, communion breakfasts, and lines of publicity in the newspapers. But American Catholicism slowly is reaching a point of domination in the Church itself. When this point is reached what then will the Church be—in attitude, in practice, in teaching and preaching? What will the Pope be—the gentle Vicar of Christ on earth, leading the faithful to a deeper penetration into the radiance of God which is called love, or a vigorous leader of a militant and proselyting organization: a priest of the inner temple or a prophet preaching his convictions at the court of the king?

This is an obvious question, rising naturally from the basic confusion surrounding a symbol of authority in the inner world who becomes a symbol of authority in the outer world. There should be no reason for such a question to come up. The Pope should never have become a power in the outer world; his position in society is that of an influence, not of a ruler. If the function of religion had continued pure he would have remained the head of an organization devoted to the inner world, to the redemption of man. The Church's dogma is the architecture of redemption; its sacramentalism is the means by which dogma is kept dynamic, so that redemption proceeds. The technique is available for any Catholic, and it is arranged so that he can employ it to his own taste and inclination, proceeding at his own speed and with whatever degree of intensity is natural to him, in the only business which is really of any concern to him, the discovery of himself and the discovery of God. That is enough work for any Church—the redemption of man. Beside it any adventures in secularism, however great, are a waste of time.

But these adventures have occurred, and they happen still. They have nothing to do with my redemption, yet as a Catholic I am expected to condone them and even to take part in them. As a Catholic, for example, I am expected by my co-religionists to approve the idea of sending an American ambassador to the Vatican. I don't. I see no good that such an ambassador can do for anyone. His existence will upset non-Catholics. It will revive old suspicions of the Pope's plans and hopes. It will cheer an already over-truculent element in American Catholicism. The combination of these two effects will produce a widening of the already wide breach between Catholics and non-Catholics, and stimulate a deepening of the already deep distrust with which the two groups regard each other.

The advantages of such an ambassador as they were presented by President Truman and as they were enlarged upon by Catholics who publicly defended the nomination, are painful to contemplate if one thinks of the Church as a religious instrument engaged in a spiritual mission. The Vatican, the President said, is the world's best "listening post," and since the Church and the United States are both fighting Communism the two should exchange such information as each possesses about the common enemy. Francis Cardinal Spellman, Archbishop of New York, endorsed these points by saying that "the United States and the Holy See have identical objectives of peace." The Protestant reaction to this presentation was realistic; in a careful examination of each point *The Christian Century*,[4] a Protestant weekly of intelligence, came to some logical conclusions. If information received at the Vatican is political rather than religious, and if the Holy See is interested in passing it on to her ally the United States, there is an American Embassy in Rome which will gladly receive callers from

[4] "An Ambassador to the Vatican?" Nov. 7, 1951.

the bishop of Rome, who is the Pope. President Roosevelt's personal representative at the Vatican, Mr. Myron C. Taylor, used the Embassy as his headquarters. Mr. Taylor's mission lasted ten years and produced nothing of value so far as is known. It would be an unreasonable outlay of the American taxpayer's money, therefore, to establish another embassy in Rome just to maintain liaison with the Vatican. If it is a matter of recognizing the Vatican as a foreign state the Pope becomes then a foreign ruler, and all members of the American Catholic hierarchy, each of whom took an oath of allegiance to him, are thus foreign agents. The American tradition of separation of Church and State—resting on the statement in the Bill of Rights (our first Amendment to the Constitution) that "Congress shall make no law respecting an establishment of religion"—would be violated by such an ambassadorship because the latest definition of this tradition, given by the Supreme Court in 1947 in the New Jersey case involving bus transportation for Catholic children attending parochial school, stated that:

> The "establishment of religion" clause of the First Amendment means at least this: Neither a state nor the Federal Government can set up a church. Neither can pass laws which aid one religion, aid all religions, or prefer one religion over another. . . . No tax in any amount, large or small, can be levied to support any religious activities or institutions, whatever they may be called, or whatever form they may adopt to teach or practice religion. Neither a state nor the Federal Government can, openly or secretly, participate in the affairs of any religious organizations or groups and *vice versa.* In the words of Jefferson, the clause against establishment of religion by law was intended to erect "a wall of separation between Church and State."

Alfred E. Smith, a Catholic governor of New York, when he was Democratic candidate for President in 1928, affirmed the Jeffersonian point of view as his own and that of the Church. Since then there have been Catholic attacks on it, based upon an interpretation which would allow the government to help religions and churches, but with equal assistance for all, giving none more aid than another. This interpretation was rejected by the Supreme Court in 1948 in the famous McCollum case, concerning released time for religious training in public schools in the town of Champaign, Illinois. Even if this interpretation were approved by the Court and accepted as practice in the United States, however, the establishment of an embassy at the Vatican would be illegal; it would favor one religion over all others.

The ring of Protestant reasoning thus closes on the idea of a Vatican ambassador at the gate of every argument. If the plan is approved by Congress it will violate the Constitution, imperil the citizenship of American Catholic bishops, and testify that the Vatican is, as *The Christian Century* says, the center of an "international spy ring." The position in which these three results will place the average American Catholic in the mind of his non-Catholic neighbor is not difficult to imagine and not pleasant to consider.

Yet none of this—none of it at all—would have come up were there no sectarianism, and there would be no sectarianism had not the totalitarian system of the inner life, the monarchy of the mystical world, extended itself to the outer world and threatened with its spiritual power the political right of free men to live freely in a free world. That was the first tragedy. The second, which came after the Western Christian church was split, was the ostentatious habit, adopted by both Protestants and Catholics, of demonstrating religion socially, so that one group might see how zealously another served God. What should have been carried secretly on the inside was worn flagrantly on the outside. Western Christian society became materially prosperous and spiritually pauperized. The late Simone Weil, a natural mystic who was born a Jewess and who came gradually in her thinking close to the heart of Catholicism, could not accept baptism because of this perversion of spirituality to social posturing. In her essay, "Forms of the Implicit Love of God," she said:

> The trap of traps, the almost inevitable trap, is the social one. Everywhere, always, in everything, the social feeling produces a perfect imitation of faith, that is to say perfectly deceptive. This imitation has the great advantage of satisfying every part of the soul. That which longs for goodness believes it is fed. That which is mediocre is not hurt by the light; it is quite at its ease. Thus everyone is in agreement. The soul is at peace. But Christ said that he did not come to bring peace. He brought a sword, the sword that severs in two, as Aeschylus says.
>
> It is almost impossible to distinguish faith from its social imitation. All the more so because the soul can contain one part of true faith and one of imitation faith. It is almost but not quite impossible.
>
> Under present circumstances, it is perhaps a question of life or death for faith that the social imitation should be repudiated.[5]

But we are not repudiating it. We are instead extending, deepening and strengthening it. We are becoming even less spiritual, and we need therefore to be more social in our religion, more dramatic in our public declarations of belief in God and submission to His commands. The burden of sectarianism is thus more heavy on our hearts; the conscience burns when it knows God is betrayed, and when the conscience burns he who owns it must either suffer himself or force someone to suffer for him.

We are not becoming more spiritual; we are growing more materialistic. We are greedy and we are afraid, and our conscience burns. We do not want to suffer in the flesh, and we refuse to suffer in the spirit. Someone else must suffer for us. With sectarianism that is easy. The other fellow will suffer for us—he who does not worship God as we do—the Jew, the Catholic, the Protestant. He is different from us, who are like

[5] Simone Weil, *Waiting for God* (G. P. Putnam's Sons, 1951), p. 198.

unto God, being made in His image. He has defied us, and by this sign defied God. He will suffer eventually at God's hands, so why not now at ours? Perhaps he will have to die.

It sounds unreal but it is so. In America we are greedy, afraid, and sectarian, and we are rich, powerful and self-righteous. Before we save the world we may strangle in our own web of evil.

This then would disappear if we gave up our sect and became all of us — Jews or Catholics, or Episcopalians or Quakers or Baptists or Presbyterians or etc

# PART TWO

Since its beginning the American Catholic Church has been a problem both to Rome and to the Protestant population of the United States. The Popes have worried because of its tendency to be American; the Protestants have watched with uneasiness its devotion to the Holy See. In the infant days of the republic, when he first took command of the Continental Army, Washington found it necessary to warn his troops against participating in anti-Catholic demonstrations. He wrote:

> As the Commander-in-Chief has been apprised of a design formed for the observance of that ridiculous and childish custom of burning the effigy of the Pope, he cannot help expressing his surprise that there should be officers and soldiers in the army so devoid of common sense as not to see the impropriety of such a step. It is so monstrous as not to be suffered or excused. Indeed instead of offering the most remote insult, it is our duty to address public thanks to our Catholic brethren, as to them we are indebted for every late success over the common enemy in Canada.[1]

Thus at the nation's birth, before the colonists had shaken off the harness of George III's rule, the Catholic problem was present and pressing. What was to be thought of a man who demonstrated a strong and courageous political loyalty to the

[1] Quoted from William Teeling, *Pope Pius XI and World Affairs* (Frederick A. Stokes Company, 1937), p. 118.

country of his residence, but who maintained at the same time affiliation with a religious system governed by a stranger dwelling in a strange land—a stranger practicing temporal as well as spiritual power, and admittedly desirous of enlisting all mankind under the banner of his Church?

Except in Maryland, Catholics had not been numerous among the colonies (in total they numbered only twenty-five thousand at the time of the Revolution), and in the republic they remained a negligible minority until the middle and late nineteenth century, when immigration collaborated with the industrial revolution to load American cities and mill towns with Italians, Germans, Irish and Slavs of a dozen nations. Three characteristics defined the majority of these newcomers: they were foreign, they were poor, and they were Catholic. These attributes, striking the native Protestant mind together, had a tendency to mingle and to emerge as a single fact—Catholics were poor foreigners who came to America to get rich. The result was a mixed set of discriminatory feelings which acted haphazardly against anyone who looked as if he were too recently off a boat. The Irish were rather often a target for these feelings, since they, though obviously foreign, spoke English as if they owned the language, and with regard to the Yankees carried chips on their shoulders eight feet high—chips placed there by four hundred years of Irish hardship under Protestant English rule. They were also, along with the Italians, the largest in numbers among the immigrants, and their clergy, commanding a fine English and being accustomed to Protestantism as an adversary, became spokesmen for both the immigrant and the Church, helping to mate the two in the Protestant mind. When I was a boy there were Irish-Americans still living who remembered seeing, when they first came to the United States, signs which read: "Men Wanted. No Irish Need Apply."

The acute aspect of this phase of discrimination did not last overlong. America was too busy, too prosperous, too much in need of strong backs and willing hands to hold a prejudice with enthusiasm or to nourish snobbery with vigor. The situation, in fact, gradually reversed itself; America became the melting pot of democracy, and its symbol changed from a trio of heroes in "the Spirit of '76" to a Jew and an Irishman doing a vaudeville skit in dialect. Then this situation, too, gradually changed; dialect became unsavory to second-generation Americans, and men whose grandfathers had been immigrants looked askance at refugees from Hitler's Germany and from Stalin's Russia.

First of all, of course, the immigrant shed his identification with poverty; he worked hard, saved his money, bought a house, and educated his children. That left him different from native Americans in only one way: he was still Catholic, and the more he became an American the more his Catholicism stuck out. For Protestants it seemed to protrude, at times, like the butt of a pistol from the pocket of a well-tailored suit. It was out of sight, and its owner was polite, but it was there.

Rome's point of view, on the other hand, was opposite to this. As American Catholics became more American it seemed to the Vatican that their Catholicism was less and less detectable. They built a lot of churches and created new parishes and dioceses, but as members of a mystical religion they seemed overly concerned with money and sex, asking continuously for one and condemning continually the other. Love of money—even money for the erection of cathedrals—is the root of all evil, and prolonged concentration on one sin, particularly the old scapegoat sin of lust, is normally an indication that other sins are being covered up. A man who is consorting with the first two of the Seven Deadly Sins, pride and covetousness, is very apt to turn attention from himself by pointing his finger at the third Deadly Sin, which is lust. It seemed to the Holy See that American Catholicism was up to something, and that this something was a tendency to drift away from the basic reason for the existence of the Church, the redemption of human souls.

In his apostolic letter on "Americanism" therefore, Leo XIII spoke against a trend among certain Catholics to neglect the strict spiritual disciplines necessary for development of the inner life, and to substitute for them actions, however worthy, in the outer world. "New methods he felt might be employed, but he did not think it safe to discard the old ones, and the natural virtues of strength and strenuousness should not be considered superior to Faith and Charity, nor were the new ideas of progress and liberty to outmode such virtues as poverty, obedience, and chastity."[2]

It was all very politely stated, and His Holiness "specifically excluded from the condemnation American political institutions and those national characteristics common to the American people as a nation."[3] The letter was addressed to Cardinal Gibbons of Baltimore and to the American hierarchy in general. Cardinal Gibbons replied that no American bishop held or taught such notions as the letter condemned, and that was all that happened. There the matter lay and there it has lain since then; no other Pope has spoken about it, however he might like to have done so. The talk of money and of sex continued, and young American priests in Rome shocked the faithful by playing tennis in white flannels. Rome took certain preventive measures and hoped for the best.

Cardinal Gibbons had moved naturally into a position of leadership in the American hierarchy; his successors were not made Cardinals, apparently lest a tradition of leadership develop around one see and provide a focus for nationalist tendencies among the bishops. The organized body of American bishops, the National Catholic Welfare Conference, was for a time banned by Pope Pius XI. When he relented and the group

[2] *Ibid.*, p. 160.

[3] Vergilius Ferm, ed., *An Encyclopedia of Religion* (The Philosophical Library, 1945), pp. 17-18.

was allowed to continue its existence, certain meaningful restrictions were placed on it:

> First, that it should be entirely voluntary for all; second, the bishops should not meet too often, not even necessarily once a year; third, that nothing should be discussed against Canon Law; fourth, that the minutes should be sent to Rome; and fifth, that no one should be given power to act for the bishops for a longer period than until the next meeting.[4]

At present the bishops, as everyone knows, meet once a year. Meanwhile the number of them grows, as the number of American Catholics grows, and the burden of supporting the Vatican falls increasingly on these American Catholics and on these bishops, who govern the dispensation of their diocesan funds.

It was not to be expected, of course, that an American Catholicism would develop without incorporating into itself certain traits of the American personality. The Spicks and Micks, the Wops and Frogs, the Hunkies and Polacks, were served at first by priests sent from the countries they had left, and for a time the Catholicism of these countries was reproduced by the immigrant groups. The intensely sentimental Catholicism of Spain; the fiercely Puritanical Catholicism of Ireland; the relaxed and affectionate Catholicism of Italy; the reasonable and sophisticated Catholicism of France; the deeply devotional Catholicism of Hungary and Poland—all were displayed in American parishes. But they lasted only until the children of the immigrants were grown and the foreign-born clergy gave way to native-born priests and bishops. Then the natural American desire to "make good," to be a success, asserted itself; an ambition to win social acceptance, to become prominent in the professions and the arts, to achieve political power, leaked into the congregations and infected the clergy.

The son of an immigrant grew up in the belief that he had

[4] *Pope Pius XI and World Affairs*, p. 161.

but one worth-while legacy—a religion superior to all others. In his youth he wore this belief as a shield; often he heard his mother say, "We must stick to our religion; it is all we have." As he grew up he wanted other things—money and prestige and acceptance by the ruling class of his community. In proportion to his achievement of these he used his Catholicism either more as a shield or less. If he failed as a person it was because the non-Catholic powers of the community were against him as a Catholic; as a Catholic he was religiously superior to all of them, but he could not conquer them single-handed on their own ground, in the world of goods and money, where they were strongly entrenched. He needed the help of other Catholics. Catholics ought to stick together in these matters. Catholics ought to vote together, in order to get political power, to elect Catholics to office, to influence government, to win for Catholics the right to prove—through political favoritism if necessary—that they were as good as anybody else, and probably better.

This was the development which caused worry to both Rome and the Protestants of America. If a Catholic expressed his religion by the way he voted, and if he voted to get himself power and prestige in the social world, he wasn't much of a Catholic and he wasn't much of a citizen. That fact was demonstrated once and for all, and with startling effects, by the strange case of Father McGlynn, which in the late eighties and early nineties cut Catholic America in two and for a time threatened Rome with the possibility of a schism.

Father McGlynn, whose Christian name was Edward, was a good and brilliant priest who was politically sympathetic to the ideas of Henry George, father of the Single Tax theory. He was pastor of St. Stephen's Church in New York on the mid-west side of Manhattan. He made speeches in favor of the Single Tax, and these came to the attention of Archbishop Michael Corrigan, his superior. Archbishop Corrigan asked

Father McGlynn to stop these talks; Father McGlynn answered that he was speaking as a citizen, that he was expressing himself solely on political subjects, and that his conduct therefore did not come under the archbishop's jurisdiction. He continued to speak for the Single Tax and the archbishop changed his request to an order. Father McGlynn defied the order and Archbishop Corrigan excommunicated him. The excommunication was confirmed in Rome, and the protest against it was so immediate and so angry that Leo XIII invited the condemned priest to the Vatican to discuss the matter.

Father McGlynn refused to go; the journey, he said, would be an admission of at least some guilt on his part, and there was no guilt. He had been judged as a priest for his actions as a citizen; the two offices, he said, priest and citizen, were independent of each other; he was not answerable to his religious superiors for what he thought or said as a citizen.

He was removed, of course, from his pastorate at St. Stephen's. When his successor preached there the collection baskets were filled with pieces of paper on which were written, "Good for 10¢ when Father McGlynn returns." All over America Catholics were angry and ready to secede from Rome; they waited only for Father McGlynn to lead them. With magnificent simplicity he told them that he could not do so. He had done no wrong, he said; he was still a priest of God, and it was up to the Pope and Archbishop Corrigan to recognize this fact. For Christ's sake, therefore, he could not lead a schism. Thousands left the Church anyhow—there are Protestant families in my home town today which were Catholic until this episode—but the thirst for schism died when the only man who could have slaked it refused to do so.[5]

Eventually some objective evidence reached the Vatican and Leo XIII sent an Apostolic Delegate to America to hear the

[5] The Story of Father McGlynn is told in Stephen Bell's, *Rebel, Priest and Prophet* (Devin-Adair Company, 1937).

case. The Delegate went to Washington and invited Father McGlynn to call on him. The priest did so, and in twenty minutes he was back in the Church. He had been right all the time, and now Archbishop Corrigan had the onerous job of reinstating him as a priest and assigning him to a parish. He sent him to Newburgh, the remotest spot in the Archdiocese of New York; there Father McGlynn served until his death in 1900. The Apostolic Delegate remained in Washington, and a Delegate has been there ever since. And ever since, as Leo XIII demonstrated by his letter to Cardinal Gibbons, the bishops of America have been under suspicion.

This was the Church into which I was baptized in 1907. The Irish clergy ran it; they dominated its organization, its hierarchy, and its point of view; they set the pattern which oriented newcomers first to Americanism, then to American Catholicism. They were disliked and resented—quietly—by priests of the other immigrant groups, who came from countries in which the aristocracy and the intelligentsia traditionally stood guard over the natural inclination of the clergy to exploit its relationship with the peasant classes, and who therefore were accustomed to performing their religious duties and to leaving well enough alone otherwise.

This had not for a long time been so in Ireland, where at the time of the Counter Reformation priests offered the sympathy and assistance of Rome to Red Hugh O'Neill and his feudal chieftains, who were fighting the Protestant armies of Queen Elizabeth. Catholicism in Ireland after Red Hugh's defeat in the battle of Kinsale became something different than it is in any other place and among any other people—it was transformed into a national religion tied to chronic political rebellion against a non-Catholic conqueror. The aristocracy and the intelligentsia of Ireland after O'Neill's defeat became largely Anglo-Irish and Protestant, and for the Catholic Irish, especially the tenant farmers who worked land owned by absentee

English landlords, the priest became everything—aristocrat, intellectual and spiritual director all in one. Rome, necessarily on the side of authority, sided with England when there were rebellions in Ireland, and Irish priests were supposed to stay out of the "troubles," but they never did. They were loyal to the Vatican generally, however, though they regarded the Italian people as a pagan lot who thought they could skip Mass because they were "the Pope's cousins."

This prudish opinion sprang, along with others, from the basic Irish dislike of becoming involved in life, from the fear in a certain type of Irishman that he will love life and embrace it passionately. He has the qualities for this involvement and this embrace, but he is inclined to reject them, making of himself, as a result, a Puritan, a quick-tempered and sometimes violent person, a whiskey drinker, a man inclined to marry late or not at all, and a fellow ready to hire out as a keeper of the law or a punisher of the sinful. It is not an overly numerous type, but it is highly noticeable. Because most people do the things he will not allow himself to do, this type takes pride in his not-doing, becoming a negative Christian. But what he wants he wants badly—freedom, self-government, the respect of others, and a decent living.

The Irish priests who came to the United States were thus admirably equipped. They were in complete command of a people who in large number were eager for everything that is termed "American," a people inclined and trained to deny, to discipline and to harness the outer world, as did the Puritans, by way of a substitute for the spiritual conquest of the inner world they were reluctant to undertake—but which their Church said was man's primary obligation in life. They fitted quickly and easily into the American cultural pattern, the pattern of education as a means of getting ahead. Because of the language barrier, members of other immigrant groups could not follow them immediately in the plunge into Americanism, so for a while the Irish Catholics and the Protestant Yankees faced each other as newcomers and natives. The first generation born of the other immigrant groups, however, joined easily and quickly the pattern set by the Irish, and Catholicism, by this curious development, became a sort of counter-Americanism—with an Irish flavor—aimed at competition with Protestantism for the fruits of the land and of the society which both inhabited. The Irish were only unhappy at being among Protestants; they hadn't wanted Protestants in Ireland and they took it for granted that Protestants didn't want them here.

The realization in childhood that I was part of this odd mixture of racial and religious prejudice brought a pain which burned and choked me, and which came back to burn and choke me for years and years, until its anguish became unbearable. I suffered it first when I was less than seven; I began to hear what came to be familiar phrases: "those people," "the Prods," "our own kind," "they don't want us." I became aware that we did not live in a community of friendly neighbors, but that as Catholics we were camped instead in the middle of warlike Protestants, who didn't want us and wouldn't let us "get ahead." We were too smart for them, so they held us back and kept us down. They disagreed with us about God, too, and they were wrong; they thought He was easygoing and kind, but He was not; He was dark and unhappy and He spent a lot of time issuing punishments to women who wore immodest costumes, to parents who did not send their children to parochial schools, and to any who did not contribute generously to the annual collection for winter coal.

Every bit of this was anathema to me, along with something special which was added to it—the folk theology of Irish Catholic women. I was forbidden to do certain things not for any understandable reason, but because, the women said, God wouldn't like me if I did. Fortunately, whatever of God I am in this life to know I discovered early; I knew His companionship from the time I could think, and I asked Him about the things I was told. He told me they were nonsense, and that the bushy-browed priests, except when they were saying Mass and reading the Gospel, were up to things He didn't understand. He comforted me, and I took none of the nonsense seriously, but I suffered from it, for as I grew older I found it had power in the world outside my mind; it could ruin my life socially.

When I was twelve a Protestant boy invited me to join the Boy Scouts. "Ask your mother if I may take you to the next meeting," he said. I asked my mother and she said no. "They don't want you," she added, "they're all Protestants." The pain was so deep when I heard this that afterward I could not bear even to look at a Boy Scout. I became a lone woodsman, hiking into the hills by myself. About this time too I began to hear the phrase, "They have everything." The Protestants, of course, were "they." The translation of the phrase was simple; what the Irish Catholic who spoke it really meant was, "I want everything."

If the Protestants were not supposed to want me, I was not supposed to want the Italians, who were allegedly inferior as people and as Catholics to the Irish; an attempt at marriage between an Irish boy and an Italian girl so shocked the Irish of the parish that the affair was broken up. This, to me, was nonsense *de luxe;* I deliberately went to all parts of the town, and made friends with Italian, Swedish, Yankee, Polish, and Lithuanian boys. But when in adolescence I made friends with Yankee and Swedish girls I encountered defeat; Protestant parents know that in mixed marriage the Catholic usually wins, since his Church insists that children of the union be brought up in the Roman faith. I was told by the Yankee and Swedish girls that they had been forbidden to date me. I was getting old enough to be dangerous. It was time, according to the custom of my people, that I went off to a Catholic college and got a "good" Catholic education.

The idea choked me. Catholic colleges—even the Jesuits admitted this—were not maintained at a high educational level, and there were far too many of them competing for the available Catholic students. Their purposes, too, did not suit me; they prepared young men to make good in the learned professions, and conditioned them to live their lives as part of a Catholic group, separated from other groups, insisting on participation in all the privileges of citizenship but acting only in the interest of their particular group.

I went instead to a nonsectarian school, where my roommate was a Baptist from Alabama who planned to enter the ministry. He thought priests demanded money from dying Catholics for the service of praying them out of hell—an abuse of the sacrament of Extreme Unction practiced by certain of the minor clergy in Luther's time—and he had heard some other odd things, not only about Catholics, but about New Englanders and Irishmen. We loved each other as brothers, we talked day and night about religion, and we did not quarrel once. We took a Presbyterian into our discussions, and the three of us ran a bull session on God which lasted without interruption for two years. We are friends yet, we three, and we belong still to the same denominations, probably because we discovered then, together, that no man is truly religious until he takes up within himself the burden of his redemption, and that when this happens all denominations fall away and the soul is alone with God.

I have known for a long time that had I gone to a Catholic college I would have left the Church. For one thing, I could not have put up with its paradoxical obsession with regard to America—separation from it as a social group, participation in it when something material is to be gained. For another, I would not have found the mysticism I needed and wanted. Protestants introduced me to *The Cloud of Unknowing*, to Brother Lawrence and Juliana of Norwich, to St. John of the

Cross and St. Teresa of Ávila, to Plotinus and Dionysius the False Areopagite; among Catholics, lay or cleric, I never heard of them. They are the heart of Catholicism; they are its mystical core; after I had found them and studied them I would not have left the Church under any persuasion; they made the system of dogma and sacraments understandable as a technique of redemption, and the technique, I discovered as I looked through the mystical literature of other religions and other peoples, was as old as the idea of finding God.

A few years ago I was in Israel in the spring, and from Galilee I went up to Jerusalem for the Passover season and for Easter. I wanted to receive Communion on Easter Sunday, so I sent word asking if one of the Franciscan fathers at Terra Sancta College might come to hear my confession. The college was not far away but I could not easily reach it because the streets were steep and I was in a wheel chair. Word came back that a monk would come to me. When by Good Friday he had not arrived I sent word again, asking this time if I might call at the college. The answer was no; I was to remain at home and a monk would reach me before Sunday morning. By Sunday noon he had not come and I gave up. That afternoon a Jewish friend rolled me to a field near the Arab-Israeli truce lines, and from there I saw the dome of the Holy Sepulchre in the Old City and heard its bells ringing for Vespers. What needed to pass between myself and God passed there, and I was at peace.

On my way home I passed the college, and for a moment I was tempted by the sight of it (the students were long gone and the monks had no duties except to themselves) to dismiss the Church as a tired and moribund presumption, too self-bemused to bother with anything but its real estate and its special privileges. But the moment passed; I had been on the Mount of Beatitudes and in the Garden of Gethsemane, and in the minds of mystics from Lao-tse to Mother Cabrini. What, against these, was a priest who forgot an appointment? The

Church declares that when one of her members can no longer believe in her he is bound in conscience to desert her; so long as she remained an instrument of redemption, so long as she led the faithful up infinitely graduated steps toward God, I did not think my conscience would tell me to go.

The search for God is a game of love; the Lover and the beloved, God and the soul, seek each other in continuous dalliance, one seeming to resist while the other attacks, then attacking while the other resists. Because the end is certain and destructively ecstatic the reaching of it is made into a deliberately delayed, deliberately frustrating, quietly joyous combat, during which nothing whatever of any sort matters except the divine wrestlers themselves. The magic of it is that the soul, as it touches the arms of its Lover, finds it is touching the universe; and that God, as His grasp closes on the beloved, takes to Himself all that He has created.

The mystic is therefore by nature an antinomist; he has used system, dogma and discipline to bring his soul into the Lover's presence, but immediately then these aids are of little use to him, though he recognizes that they must be maintained in order that others may also employ them as a ladder to the sight of God. The unfortunate point is that fewer and fewer among the Catholic laity—and among the secular clergy also—use the system, dogma and disciplines of the Church for this high purpose, but treat them as if they were ends in themselves. With their true meaning hidden, ignored or unexplained, therefore, they seem to non-Catholics—and even to many Catholics—to be irrational and unnecessary. The accretions which cling to them, the social structure of the Church and its political activity, seem also irrational and unnecessary, and mystics outside the Church find that though their eyes are on the true meaning of the system, dogma and disciplines, their will to use them is trapped by the outer obstacles of the Church's nonreligious, nonmystical activities.

Simone Weil, in explaining why she could not bring herself to be baptized, referred to what she termed the Church's "patriotism"–its exclusiveness historically and socially, its insistence on a monopoly in salvation, its cushioning of weak egos by allowing them to say "we" instead of "I."[6] A soul must go from "we" to "I" before it can find its relationship with God, and she knew this; she was already an "I" and in spirit she was at the center of the Church's mystical being, but she was afraid she might lose that "I" if she entered the Church formally, through the outer gate around which the bazaars and markets and curio shops are arranged. I consider, when I think of Simone Weil, that I was fortunate to be born inside the gate, and that I was lucky in having the sense to take myself inward toward the center in my flight from the noise of the markets, instead of fleeing outward through the gate.

But a member of the Church, however he may himself feel, cannot ignore the noise of his comrades within the gates, or the impression their conduct makes on those who are without. The old feeling among American Catholics of not belonging and of not being wanted has developed now into a separatist tendency which displays itself in an increasing number of organizations, institutions and committees whose title begins with the word "Catholic." The habit among Irish clergy of acting as aristocrats and intelligentsia for their congregations has developed into a system of supervision and censorship for literature, the arts and entertainment; the American Catholic who reads his diocesan paper, for example, discovers a list of the plays and movies he may not see, and of the books he is not free to read.

Unfortunate as these situations are in themselves their real danger lies in the attempt which is made to fasten them on the non-Catholic population. When a member of the hierarchy

[6] *Op. cit.*, pp. 52-53.

condemns a book or play or movie and calls on all Catholics to boycott the condemned item, the collective power of Catholicism is being used to threaten a publisher or producer or theater owner with economic ruin unless he withdraws from the market something a bishop dislikes. In a smaller way Catholic groups and organizations badger newspaper and magazine editors, and the producers and sponsors of radio and television shows. Any mention of anything Catholic must be favorable or the heat is on; an unfavorable comment brings hundreds of letters, abusing the author of the comment and threatening the editor with boycott of his publication. Often I review Catholic books; if I find one which is poor, and if I say it is poor, I am certain to get a bundle of letters beginning, "You dirty Protestant . . ."

If this sort of pressure were a failure it would be well for the Catholics. Unfortunately for them it succeeds. It is economic, and the publishers who govern the editors cannot resist it; nor can the men who produce plays, movies, and radio and television shows. Consequently, all over the country editors and publishers, producers and directors, authors and agents, are turning sour on Catholicism. If Catholic pressure and Catholic censorship continue in the future to succeed as they have in the recent past, the Church in America will be set back two hundred years, back to the times of the burning of the Pope in effigy.

It would benefit American Catholics a great deal if they could see themselves as other Catholics see them—Catholics in Europe, for example, who think of all Americans as rich adolescents, and who regard American Catholics as an irreligious lot of moneygrubbers. In the past twenty-four months two long studies of American Catholicism have appeared in French publications. In the newspaper *Le Monde*, in a series of articles published on January 10, 11, and 12, 1950, George Escoulin said:

The anxiety to "be accepted" has led American Roman Catholics to adopt the habits, the customs and the vision of the American world without analyzing them in the light of their own faith. . . . In the deportment and in the deep-seated reactions of the Roman Catholics it is very difficult to discern the essential characteristics of Christian bearing.

Mr. Escoulin also said:

In the field of domestic affairs as in that of international relations it may be said that the positions taken by American Roman Catholics are largely determined by the following fact: they live their Church above all as a *sociological reality*. And in saying that *they live* rather than *they think* a distinction of capital importance is intended. The problem which now remains to be solved is that of living their Church, increasingly, as a *spiritual reality*, while carefully preserving those roots which not merely enabled them to protect their faith in a setting which was either hostile or indifferent, but also caused them to command respect for it and promote its growth.

In the Catholic Action magazine *Au Service De Tous* for January, 1951, a group study reported:

The result for which the American Church was striving has been achieved: it is at present very wealthy and its faithful are citizens esteemed by their compatriots. Catholicism has become the religion of a large portion of the Middle Class . . . it is dominated by the Irish clergy. . . . The result has been . . . a magnificent cohesion of all American Catholics, but also an exploitation of the Church by the Irish to form a kind of club, a kind of friendly association with a bureau which has as its goal to keep intact the status of its founders and to initiate new immigrants into the American way of life rather than to let them radiate a way of life and to "Catholicize" America.

The report continues:

The Catholics make up a sociological entity, a well-knit group, where there is unity and even strength, but which does not shine forth with vitality, being too intent upon its own internal problems. Its endeavors are numerous, prosperous and remarkable from several points of view, but they remain "administrative" and without influence for the world outside. . . . The American parish very often gives the impression of power and especially of wealth: attendance at Mass is high, the church is spacious and comfortable, the schools are flourishing, the endeavors successful; the Irish priest reigns there with authority, lives very graciously, even in luxury, and is highly regarded in the community; he sees to it that the schools fulfill well their function, which is the formation of American Catholics. But this parish remains more a social group than anything else, a group which must give an impression of greater and greater power for fear of losing all advantages thus far gained in its pursuit of social elevation.

In the economic and social sphere, the contribution of the Catholics has been until now very slight. Their extreme nationalism causes them to sequester themselves in a fearful conservatism and they have become the most ardent defenders of capitalism. Their super-patriotism has often hindered them from taking a stand definitely in important questions. Practically never, for example, have they dared approach the Negro question, a crucial problem in the United States. . . .

They combat Communism, of course, but as Americans in the field of politics, and not as Catholics waging a doctrinal battle. This has led them to accept, even to make use of, certain extremist methods or certain propaganda of doubtful orthodoxy (for example, in the case of the Committee of un-American Activities). Everything presented to them as American is sure to win their approbation without discrimination. The result is even a kind of complete disinterestedness concerning the problems of the world: at the time when Cardinal Mindszenty was sentenced, there was strong reaction among the clergy, but this was more a defensive reaction than one of inquiry. It did not even inspire objective inquiries into the situation in other countries.

American Catholics with all their effort have succeeded thus only in more firmly impaling themselves on the horns of their dilemma. Their brethren abroad regard them as materialistic Americans; their non-Catholic neighbors at home consider them belligerently withdrawn in social matters, unco-operative in communal activities, separatist in social welfare, clannish in politics, and insufferably arrogant in everything which pertains to religion. Their clergy will not join with the clergy of other faiths in any endeavor, however nonreligious (exceptions to the rule are so widely publicized that everyone hears of them and thinks they happen often). A Catholic convert of any prominence is welcomed into the Church with the discreet tumult of a gangster's funeral; if he can write or talk he is then put to work as a propagandist, and if his life story ends as a best seller everyone is happy. He has been thoroughly converted to "we." Meanwhile, nothing whatever is said about the heavy leakage in Church membership—Catholics who join other sects; Catholics who stop taking the sacraments; Catholics who avoid the confessional because they are using birth control in marriage, or have become addicted to some other sin they cannot give up—unholy love, or the gluttony of alcohol.

All of this is not necessary and none of it is helpful, either to Catholicism or to Protestantism (which has its own types of exclusiveness, separatism, social snobbery, and religious arrogance). Mostly, however, it is not helpful to the United States; it is—in combination with the sectarian separatism of Protestantism—the largest single force for disunity in the nation. It is one of the few influences which separate Americans socially, and among these it affects the largest number of people in the greatest number of ways. It injures our co-ordination as a people; it divides our efforts as Christians in the outer world of charity and benevolence; it gives us loneliness and misgiving within ourselves; it makes our entire democracy ill from lack of spiritual circulation; it sets us against one another in trivial matters when we should be together in affairs of importance; it punctuates with a question mark our statement that we are Christians.

Any Catholic knows the remedy for it; if he used his religion as it should be used, to govern and to discipline and to sanctify his inner life, it would not be necessary for him to project that inner life into his social existence, where it designates him a paranoid and makes those who deal with him uncomfortable. It would not be necessary for him to knock the block off anyone who spoke slightingly of the Pope; he would not have to feel that his purpose in life is to keep the world from speaking a word against his Church. He would realize that the Church's totalitarian system is an image of the inner world he must develop for himself, and he would know that if he is to develop that inner world he must first of all have freedom in his outer world—freedom to seek his redemption in peace and security. That would make him the best possible Catholic and the best possible American; that would prove that the outer life and the inner life are interdependent, each needing the peace of the other for its own peace. That would prove that the secure and harmonious life this country seeks to give its inhabitants is impossible while those inhabitants are inwardly irreligious and outwardly sectarian.

Yet that is the way things are and that is the way they obviously are going to remain. When a thing has happened it is too late to blame anyone. It is of no consequence which came first in this matter, the Catholic feeling of "not belonging" or the Protestant suspicion of Catholic "foreignness"; both came into being, are fully grown, and may become rampant. Nor is it important, at least from a practical viewpoint of dealing with the situation, how the Catholic side became Irish-flavored. It may occur to some to derive from the evidence a feeling that the Irish clergy might divert the threat of a sectarian crisis by changing their point of view and their tactics.

But the Irish clergy are first of all Catholics, and they are also —a fact of equal importance—American citizens. As Catholics they are criticized by their Church for being overly American, and although Protestantism regards the threat of their growing power and intransigence as primarily a Roman threat, the fact is that this threat comes from a hearty adaptation of Catholicism to the American system of free enterprise. The Catholics thus are coupled in the prejudiced mind with the Jews, who also are considered too successful, and who also are supposed to want to "run things." But the Jews are not a proselyting group, and they are not noisily orthodox in their religious practices. The Catholics are both, and whether the American Church were dominated by Irish or Italian clergy, by French bishops or Spanish Cardinals, Protestants would feel the breath of Catholic missionary zeal and hear the chimes of Catholic Masses. There would be irritation and confusion and a desire to know either *what is to be feared or why there is no reason for fear*. Even a Catholic at times suffers irritation and confusion at what goes on in his Church. In 1821 a Frenchwoman, Madame d'Agoult, wrote:

> I accepted the great mysteries of Catholicism: the Trinity, the Incarnation, the Fall, the Redemption, just because they were great: I loved the ceremonies of the cult because of their symbolic beauty; but the trifling devotions, the trifling miracles, the trifling holy picture business, the silly emblems, all the factors, all the superstitions of an idolatrous and sensual Catholicism, lowered to the level of trifling minds, invincibly repelled me.[7]

American Protestants in the present feel this same invincible repulsion, and the force of it is precisely in proportion to the lack of Catholic spirituality, which the Church's external and sentimental displays of faith emphasize by their ostentation and dramatize by their smug assumption of divine collaboration.

[7] Daniel Stern (Madame d'Agoult), *Mes Souvenirs* (Paris, 1887), p. 170.

It is not the sinner who is loathed by honest folk; it is the hypocrite. Behind the scarlet curtain of elaborate rituals, Communion breakfasts, and national conferences of lay and clerical groups, Protestants see in American Catholicism an efficiently organized, energetic, "on-the-make" pressure group which is driving toward social and political power in the United States. Meanwhile, the members of this pressure group, while remaining separated socially from all non-Catholic citizens, maintain religious allegiance to a spiritual leader who is himself a foreigner, and whose predecessors have sought and held temporal power and declared their right to hold it—and declared also that their mission, assigned to them by God, is to convert the world to their faith and to their rule. It worries the Protestants, and it should. Such a departure from the ideals of Catholicism is disquieting news for everyone; when the shepherd follows his flock while it strays, denying that it is lost so long as he is with it, there is concern among the owners of other flocks, and among the sheep themselves.

Yet this concern among Protestants would not arise if Protestantism were not also lacking in spirituality. If Protestants were practicing Christians in the original sense of this phrase the present state of American Catholicism would be looked upon as a ridiculous parody of the religion founded by Jesus, and would be treated as if it were just that. But since there is a lack of spirituality on both sides, the claims of Catholicism to alliance with God must be treated by Protestantism as possibly valid—as possibly valid as its own. That Catholicism's claims could be reduced by an exhibition of genuine Christianity on the part of Protestants, or that Protestantism's claims could be thinned down by an uprising of honest fervor among Catholics, is too apparent a solution. It is true, but it is hopeless, and therefore it is unreasonable.

The Christian world is not spiritual; it is strong, it is well-off, and it is idealistic, but it is too comfortable and too fascinated by the world it controls and exploits to be interested in making *safari* toward heaven. We are Christians by declaration, but we are not inclined to proceed with redemption. Yet since redemption *must* proceed, being the reason for man's existence, the inertia of society, when it sets in, is broken by history through just such phenomena as are assailing us now—wars and rumors of war, famine, pestilence, and confusion of minds. As a cure for spiritual malaise war is a drastic treatment, and it does not work quickly. But it works, and unless we devise a self-cure for our national anemia of the soul, and administer it, it will in our case soon be stepping up its dosage.

Meanwhile, there is no hope that from within our sectarianism we shall be able to release ourselves from the pain of its pressure. Nothing can be done about it because action means co-operation and the Catholics cannot co-operate. Many among the laity—the younger folk especially—would like to, but they have neither power nor influence with their clergy. Whatever is done must be done by parties of neither part, men and women who, though members of the separated groups, are within themselves at work on the matter of their relationship with God, and thus are free of the prejudices and taboos of social religion. Such freedom from prejudices and taboos is exhibited by members of the Catholic Worker Movement, which under the leadership of Dorothy Day has formed a bridge of understanding between Catholics and Protestants while pursuing a communal pattern of life built on the basic ideals of Christianity. Catholics in this movement try to *live* the Sermon on the Mount, and because their effort is genuine they find Protestants of all sorts coming to their meetings in the Lower East Side of New York and to retreats at their farm communities.

Such people as these are the Christian minority which can do something about sectarianism. They are the Catholics and the Protestants who look to the Sermon on the Mount for their ideal, and who try—falling a thousand times a day—to live up to that ideal. They are the men and women who go to Mass or to service on Sunday but who also carry their religion into Monday, feeling it in their hearts and expressing it in their thoughts and in their deeds. They are the church members of all sects and of all religions who believe in fulfilling the law of God in its spiritual, not in its physical, sense.

They are the salt of the earth, the salt which has not lost its savor. There are a few of them—but only a few—in each community in America; even in places which are blessed they are not numerous. But together they form the leaven which keeps the loaf of Christianity raised, and which prevents religion from descending—as it has a tendency to do—to the level of farce. These people, wherever two or three of them are gathered—and where therefore He is in their midst—can do something about sectarianism.

What can they do? They can pray. They can pray that the heads of their churches, charged with the spiritual welfare of a people become leaders and defenders of what remains of a free world, realize into what danger their continued noncooperation and hostility are leading us, and turn toward one another for understanding and strength, rather than away from one another in suspicion and fear.

They can do more than that. They can speak among themselves of the social unity they want and of the tolerance and friendship they desire one for the other. They can begin to bring about among themselves this social unity and these qualities of tolerance and friendship.

Something must be done, and somewhere it must begin. Why not, as a starting point, as a practical means of breaking the inertia and hesitancy which are to be expected in groups so long separated, bring together for conversation and discussion a small group of these men who realize the deep danger of sectarianism and the strong need for neutralizing its negative force? Ten would be enough for a start—five from each side of the fence. They could meet for informal conversations in the beginning, talking about anything until they became thoroughly acquainted. That process would uncover what common ground lay between them, and because they would be men of good will there would be much of this. There would be more common ground, in fact, than there would be grounds for difference; of this I am certain. It is what invariably happens when decent people become friends.

It would be no more than a start, but after that start anything and everything could happen. As Americans we are against iron curtains; we should not maintain one between ourselves, particularly one so old, so rusty, and which marks a division never intended by God to exist among men.

But what can a few Catholics and Protestants, though spiritual and of good will, do about sectarianism in its larger framework, where it involves the community and the country? Theology, a science of disagreement where sectarianism is concerned, must be removed from whatever is attempted. Any question as to who is right about what, must be deleted from the agenda. The matter of social mixing must be ignored. Above all there must be no mention of God.

That leaves only a limited area for action. Concerning that area these men of spirit and good will might make a modest proposal.

The religious disunity of Americans is social. The religious unity of Americans is also social. Whatever the sect, its expression of religious conviction is nowadays largely in the field of social welfare. In that activity there is no disagreement; each sect looks after its own, but none disapproves of what the other is about. On the battlefield of misery, in fact, soldiers from the differing camps find themselves co-operating through natural need and compulsory necessity. They could, with less effort than it takes *not* to co-operate, co-operate more. If someone with sufficient power and persuasion, free of all camps, were to lead them, they might do it, with the help of those from both sides who want such co-operation.

How this man of sufficient power and persuasion could lead them in a sense depends on who he is. If he were the President of the United States—the man who proposed sending an ambassador to Rome—he could invite leaders of welfare divisions from all sects, Jewish as well as Christian, Moslem and Hindu and Confucianist (for the faithful of these religions are numbered among us, and have their welfare problems) to meet with him and discuss a plan for co-operation in the labors which all of them practice, in the works of mercy and charity and rehabilitation which they do among the poor and the shipwrecked in life. He could ask those who did meet with him to join with him in forming a Presidential committee for devising, among social welfare divisions of all religions, a system for exchange of information and for interuse of facilities and personnel.

It is a simple idea—too simple for so complex a problem. It could be dismissed by both Catholics and non-Catholics as unnecessary, impractical, and expensive. But if it were the President's idea could such things be said? It offers the advantage of a central office dispensing information, equipment and workers to all areas of need in all religions; the central office would pay for itself in the efficiency it brought to welfare work in each religion, in its ability to eliminate overlapping of services, in the saving it would effect for individual institutions and organizations through co-operative use of equipment. It would require no more gregariousness among workers of different faiths than is required in any office or factory. But it would put people of all faiths at work together in the common business of every religion—the active love of humanity and the succor of its afflicted members.

The point is that were we a spiritual people this kind of

co-operation would long ago have sprung up spontaneously among us, and would not now have to be suggested, timidly and hesitantly and with a certainty that no one will do anything about it.

But something must be done, somehow, by someone. We cannot allow sectarianism to grow in bitterness among us when we are so threatened from beyond our limits. We should not tolerate it among us at any time, under any circumstances; it stands more strongly between us and God than the whole of the universe. We should begin to talk about it, and we should begin to do something about it.

We must begin somewhere, in some way, and since now there abides with us so little of faith and hope, we have but charity. If in this we are not brothers; if in this we are not together, then the burden of our religious separation has been carried for nothing, for as a people we do not even believe in God.